'… to those who are sanctified
in Christ Jesus,

called to be saints'

Lent 2002

CHURCHES TOGETHER
IN BRITAIN AND IRELAND

Churches Together in Britain and Ireland
Inter-Church House, 35–41 Lower Marsh
London SE1 7SA
Tel: +44 (0)20 7523 2121; Fax: +44 (0)20 7928 0010
info@ctbi.org.uk or (team)@ctbi.org.uk
www.ctbi.org.uk

Registered charity number 259688
ISBN 0 85169 252 4

Published 2001 for Churches Together in
Britain and Ireland. Produced by Church House Publishing

Further copies are available from:
CTBI Publications, 31 Great Smith Street, London SW1P 3BN
Tel: +44 (0)20 7898 1300; Fax: +44 (0)20 7898 1305;
orders@ctbi.org.uk   www.chbookshop.co.uk

Cover photographs, clockwise from top left:
St Andrew; St Brigid; Archbishop Janani Luwum; William and Catherine Booth;
St David with a harp; St Hilda; Oscar Romero (see p. 60 for acknowledgements).

Illustrations by Peter Wilks, c/o SGA
Cover design by AD Publishing Services

Typeset in 10 on 12pt Sabon by Vitaset, Paddock Wood, Kent

Printed in Great Britain by
Creative Print and Design Group, Ebbw Vale, Wales

Contents

Members of the Lent 2002 planning group

Ms Bernadette Askins   Roman Catholic Church

Revd Michele Barzey   Minority Ethnic Anglican Concerns
(attended the first meeting and made most valuable contributions but was prevented by illness from further work with the group)

Dr George Bithos   Orthodox Church

Revd Margaret Cundiff   Church of England

Ms Jeanette Dean   Christian Fellowship Church, Belfast

Revd Donald Hilton (Moderator)   United Reformed Church

Revd Martin Johnstone   Church of Scotland

Revd Kevin Scully   Church of England

Anne Smith   Religious Society of Friends

The member nominated by the Church in Wales was not able to attend or contribute to the planning group but helpful suggestions were made by Siôn Aled Owen, the General Secretary of ENFYS (The Commission of Covenanted Churches in Wales).

Mr Simon Barrow   CTBI Staff Consultant

Revd Jean Mayland   CTBI Staff Consultant

Preface

In many church traditions Lent is regarded as a time when Christians are called upon to grow in holiness. After all, the word Lent comes from the Old English word *lencten*, meaning 'spring', and spring is a time of new growth.

Through this Lent course entitled *Called to be saints*, local groups of Christians are invited to reflect on the meaning of this phrase which is found in several places in the New Testament. In response to this call we shall consider our pilgrimage together in the Christian life and listen to the stories of individuals and communities whose example can inspire and encourage us.

As groups work through this course we believe that the participants will be challenged both as individuals and as members of both church and secular communities.

May they and we also be inspired to follow in the footsteps of the saints, that we may grow in holiness and in our allegiance to the one Lord. Through our life together the world may catch some glimpse of the glory of God.

As Presidents of Churches Together in Britain and Ireland we warmly commend the Lent 2002 course to local Churches Together groups and we thank the moderator and the planning group for all their hard work.

Rt Revd Mario Conti

Rt Revd John Neill

Rt Revd Barry Rogerson

Revd Nezlin Sterling

Sister Eluned Williams

Introduction

Welcome

Welcome to the Lent 2002 study course promoted by CTBI (Churches Together in Britain and Ireland). A course is produced every two years and is widely used by local groups of Christians across the four nations of England, Ireland, Scotland and Wales. Most groups will be formed from local Churches Together groups or *ad hoc* ecumenical groups created for the purpose. Such groups studying a biblical theme together are able to learn from the insights of our different traditions. It is an ecumenical gift to reveal these to each other and an ecumenical challenge to listen to each other.

The planning group and writers who produced the course were selected by CTBI to be widely representative of the denominations and the four nations. Their several meetings were held in a spirit of co-operation and Christian fellowship. The differing emphases of the representatives were acknowledged and appreciated, and the co-operation within the group was a source of personal growth in understanding each other, and in faith. Their confidence is that as local groups follow this course they will be given the same spirit.

Called to be saints

The phrase 'called to be saints' is taken from several places in the New Testament. One reference is shown on the cover of this booklet, and another is found at Romans 1.7. In most of the greetings which form the opening verses of Paul's letters he describes his readers, the local Christians, as 'the saints'. A major aim of this five-week course is to explore the meaning of this description as a glimpse of the past, an insight into our present calling, and a challenge to prepare for the future. 'Saints' carries a meaning both for individuals and communities. It will be impossible to work through this course seriously without being challenged, both about our individual discipleship and about the nature of our church and the wider communities in which we live.

Where did the ideas for the course come from?

Three factors influenced the planning group. Together they form a back-cloth to the course against which the *Called to be saints* theme is explored.

1. The 'Building Bridges of Hope' process *(See also Appendix 1)*

BBH is a learning and sharing process for churches that are seeking creative ways of engaging with their local communities for the sake of the gospel and the common good. Initially 40 congregations across the four nations became a 'living laboratory' for other churches who wanted to be engaged in mission appropriate to our present time. The influence of that process on this course will be self-evident, especially in Session 5, and further details can be found in Appendix One.

2. A conference about the meaning of 'saint' *(See also Appendix 2)*

A conference was organized by the CTBI in Durham during November 1999. Its primary purpose was to think about Abbess Hild (Hilda) and the northern saints. Hilda was born into a noble Northumbrian family and became abbess of the double monastery, i.e. for both men and women, at Whitby in 657. The monastery was a centre of learning. She instigated the Synod of Whitby in 664 which, among other things, discussed the then divisive dating of Easter, and also the conflict between the Roman and Celtic expressions of the Christian faith. At the 1999 Durham conference this led to a wider discussion on the meaning of 'saint', which has been fed into this Lent course.

3. Christians as pilgrims *(See also Appendix 3)*

'Pilgrimage' is a familiar concept for Christians. For some it takes the form of travel to religious sites; for others it is seen more as an internal journey of personal discovery and faith development. It can be an individual journey or taken in company with others. During the year 2000 – when this course was first planned – a European pilgrim journey was taking place which began in Thessalonika, Greece, through Norway and on to the British Isles before continuing to Iasi in Romania, and Prague. Lent is itself a pilgrimage, and those who share this course will travel in company with each other. Many of those involved in this course will have worked and worshipped together during the 2001 Week of Prayer for Christian Unity, when the theme of the prayer leaflet entitled *Together on the Way* was chosen by an ecumenical group of Christians in Romania.

Setting up the Lent course

Those responsible for setting up the groups should plan early. Start thinking about it in the autumn of 2001. Use the local Churches Together as a forum for planning and ensure that all local churches are contacted. Consult local church leaders and other key people. Order the books in good time; further copies can be obtained from Church House Bookshop (see back cover). Many groups plan an evening meeting, but consider the possibility of several groups, meeting at different times of the day and on different days of the week. Lent begins when the evenings are still dark; there will be people who would prefer a meeting held during the morning or afternoon rather than the evening. A Sunday afternoon may also be possible. Circulate the list of possible times and days to encourage the greatest support. Ideally, a group should have between six and ten members. Consider the possibility of a launch meeting or service to initiate the course, especially if several groups have been planned. Alternatively, consider a final joint meeting or act of worship to draw the course to a conclusion.

Guidance for the leader

The leader of the group should read the following seven points carefully.

1. *The group meeting*

This course is designed so that a group can meet weekly for five weeks during Lent. Ideally, each member of the group should have a personal copy of the book. Each session is planned to last 90 minutes and the timing of each section is indicated in italics. The effectiveness of a group often depends on the ability of the leader to keep the session moving whilst seeming to be relaxed; that requires good preparation by the leader. If refreshments are to be offered before or after the meeting, allow extra time for this rather than making inroads into the actual session.

2. *The aim of each session*

The aim of each session is clearly given. The leader should have this in mind throughout the meeting and may also want to read it out to the group. It is followed by a brief summary of the session showing how the CTBI planning group suggests the aim can be achieved. An appropriate timing for each step in the process is indicated as a guide.

3. Preparation

> At the beginning of every session, the preparation the leader needs to make is indicated in a box like this one.

> Where the group members may also be involved in the preparation for a session, details are given at the end of the previous session in a box like this one. These are placed before the final worship in the text. Decide whether to give out these details before or after the final worship in the session.

So that the leader can be well prepared before the course begins, a list of the major practical resources required for the five sessions – apart from those provided within the pages of this book – is given below:

Session 1
- A map of the world
- A map of the local area
- Small adhesive labels and a marker pen

Note that the map of Britain and Ireland is provided on page 6 but may need to be enlarged.

Session 2
- Plain postcards
- The audio cassette of stories if one has been made (see details under *Storytelling* below)

Session 3
- Names and profiles of saints to be photocopied from this book, preferably onto thin card
- Three- to four-metre lengths of string or wool
- The cassette of stories if one has been made

Session 4
- Photographs brought by group members
- Candles or tea-lights,* pebbles, or flowers according to your choice
- A Taizé (or other) chant if one is available and you choose to use it
- The cassette of stories if one has been made

Session 5
- Four large sheets of plain paper
- A marker pen
- A candle in a stable candle-holder
- Newspaper excerpts provided by group members

* 'Tea-lights' are variously called 'table-lights' or 'night-lights'; in this booklet the name 'tea-light' is used.

4. *Storytelling*

Since this course is about people – those called to be saints – it includes many stories, especially in the Sessions 2, 3 and 4. Decide how you will handle these. If they are to be read by group members, forewarn those reading them so that they can carefully prepare them; the best story can be ruined by careless reading. Consider the possibility of taping some or all of the stories and using a cassette player in the session. Note that such a cassette of stories is not available either commercially or from CTBI; if the suggestion is taken up it must be produced locally. There may be people in one of the churches skilled in this; even someone not be able to attend the sessions but who would be glad to offer this help. Can some of the stories be used in church the previous Sunday – perhaps during all-age worship – so that people come to the group already familiar with one or more of them?

5. *Activities*

Discussion is a basic element to this course but it is often introduced by a practical activity. Decide how much time to give to discussion and how much to activity, so as to get the best advantage from both. The activities are intended to stir people's imagination so that they do not go unprepared into discussion. Encourage creativity in the group.

6. *Bible readings*

All the Bible readings are given in full, and are taken from the *New Revised Standard Version*.

7. *Worship*

However brief, the suggested worship is integral to the course. Different styles of prayers are provided from week to week; no attempt has been made to make them uniform. In part, they reflect the different traditions from which the writers come. Some groups may prefer to ignore the offered prayers and use their own, or to encourage spontaneous contributions from group members; others may want to begin times of prayer with silence. Enjoy the variety which the traditions present in the group allow.

Final words

Be faithful to the aim of the sessions but don't be afraid to adapt the material to your own situation. Be creative. Encourage spontaneity.

Would you like to share in an experiment?

Children and the Lent course

This course, like its predecessors, has been planned with adults in mind rather than children. At a late stage in its thinking the planning committee wondered if children could be involved in this and future courses. The decision was made to offer a parallel course for children this year. If it is to be continued in the future we need to know if it is wanted and would be used.

A start for Lent 2002

A simple course, based on the *Called to be saints* theme, can be found on the Internet at the CTBI website (www.ctbi.org.uk/lent). Children's leaders would need to be pointed to this possibility at an early stage to adapt what is offered to their particular circumstances.

The material takes a children's hymn, 'I sing a song of the saints of God', and invites children's groups to illustrate the hymn by making a frieze or scrapbook. Possible illustrations are suggested and appropriate stories are given. Some worship material is included. If you use this material please let us know if it was useful. Critical comments will be as welcome as commendation. We simply want to know if future planning committees should look more seriously at the possibility, and we need your advice to make the decision.

Please write to:

The Revd Jean Mayland
Churches Together in Britain and Ireland
Inter-Church House
35–41 Lower Marsh
LONDON SE1 7SA

email: jean.mayland@ctbi.org.uk

Session 1

Called to be saints: Who's called?

Aim

To widen our understanding of the meaning of 'saint'.

To achieve the aim:

- after prayer and introductions we explore Corinth and its people whom Paul called 'saints';

- then, with maps of the world, Britain and Ireland, and our own locality, and helped by biblical insights, we widen the search for saints;

- we design an advertisement, which helps us to decide what we really look for in those 'called to be saints';

- finally, we reflect on the implications of this for our own discipleship, and close with prayer.

Preparation before this session

You will need three maps, one each of:

- the world, for **Exploring Corinth** and the activity **Find the saints**, plus adhesive labels on which to write the names of places and saints in the latter;

- Britain and Ireland (see page 6), plus adhesive labels on which to write the names of places and saints in **Find the saints**; and

- your local area (town, village or suburb, etc.).

Familiarize yourself with the various maps so as to help the group quickly to find the places suggested in the course.

Welcome and introductions *(15 minutes)*

- On this first week of the course invite the members of the group briefly to introduce themselves by saying who they are, where they live, and to which church they belong.

Prayer

Almighty God,
by whose Spirit we are inspired and sanctified:
hear our prayer which we offer for your faithful people,
called to serve you in all times and places,
so that whatever they do or say,
they may serve you in holiness and truth
to the glory of your name;
through our Lord and Saviour Jesus Christ. Amen.

Adapted from the collect for Pentecost 2, *The Alternative Service Book 1980*, SPCK

- In buzz groups (two or three people talking together) invite group members briefly to mention any inspiring event or person in their lives, present or past.

Exploring Corinth

1. Visit the place *(10 minutes)*

On the map of the world (or a page of an atlas for a larger scale), turn to Greece and find the city of Corinth at the southern end of the Gulf of Corinth in Greece. Identify any other cities and regions in the eastern Mediterranean area that are important to the New Testament story.

Corinth was the centre of government and commerce in Greece, just as Athens was the centre of education. Situated on the principal sea route between Rome and the East, it was a major trade centre. A cosmopolitan port, its lax morals were proverbial.

Create a discussion around the following questions:

- What else do we know about Corinth?
- Name any people who lived in, or visited, Corinth.
- Have any members of the group ever been to Corinth themselves? If so, what did they see?
- Refer to the title of this course. Was Corinth the kind of place where you might expect to find saints?

2. Meet the church (15 minutes)

First, invite the members of the group silently to read the following extract from the early verses of Paul's letter to the church at Corinth. Then read aloud both the brief introduction and, once again, the verses of the letter.

After the expected form of greeting common to first-century letter writers, Paul rejoices both in the spiritual life of the Christians in Corinth, and in the faithfulness of God.

> *To the church of God that is in Corinth, to those who are sanctified in Christ Jesus, called to be saints, together with all those who in every place call on the name of our Lord Jesus Christ, both their Lord and ours:*
>
> *Grace to you and peace from God our Father and the Lord Jesus Christ.*
>
> *I give thanks to my God always for you because of the grace of God that has been given you in Christ Jesus, for in every way you have been enriched in him, in speech and knowledge of every kind – just as the testimony of Christ has been strengthened among you – so that you are not lacking in any spiritual gift as you wait for the revealing of our Lord Jesus Christ. He will also strengthen you to the end, so that you may be blameless on the day of our Lord Jesus Christ. God is faithful; by him you were called into the fellowship of his Son, Jesus Christ our Lord.*
>
> 1 Corinthians 1.2-9

Encourage the group to react to Paul's use of the word 'saints' for the community of faith in Corinth. (Buzz groups could be used again if the whole group is large.)

- What marks them out as 'saints' for Paul?
- What is the source of the strength of these people?
- What do these verses tell us about the nature of the church in Corinth?

Activity: Find the saints *(15 minutes)*

Recognizing the 'ordinariness' of saints, and using the three maps, one by one, ask members of the group to locate some of the places named below. They don't need to find them all. Then, in the limited time allowed, name a 'saint' from some of the places. Mark the places with a sticker, preferably bearing the saint's name. Remember that anyone can be a saint; some may be well known, others known only in the experience of one or two people in the group. Some will be historic figures; others contemporary, perhaps known through missionary and aid agencies or met on holiday visits. Some members of the group may recall their 'saint' first, and then locate the place.

Start with the map of the world, and locate:

Italy (Assisi)	Egypt	India
South Africa	France (Orleans)	Canada
Nigeria	The United States of America	Russia
Australia	Japan	Germany (Bingen)
Latin America		

Then move to the map of Britain and Ireland and do the same:

Pembrokeshire	London	Yorkshire	Cornwall
Norwich	Lindisfarne	Glasgow	Belfast
Iona	Wells	Durham	Hertfordshire

Finally, move to the map of your local community. With your new understanding of the meaning of 'saint' consider whether there is any local place, person or community that can be called saintly. Mark such places and the name(s) of the saint(s) in the same way as before.

Bible reading and discussion *(10 minutes)*

Read the following introduction and Bible passage.

Towards the end of the second century a Roman governor (Pliny) wrote that Christians were drawn from every strata of society. However, about the same time, another author (Celsus) wrote of Christians that 'we see them in their own houses: wool-dressers, cobblers, and fullers, the most uneducated and vulgar persons.' They are like 'worms in a conventicle in a corner of mud'. Around AD 55, Paul wrote to the Christians in Rome:

> *Consider your own call, brothers and sisters: not many of you were wise by human standards, not many were powerful, not many were of noble birth. But God chose what is foolish in the world to shame the wise; God chose what is weak in the world to shame the strong; God chose what is low and despised in the world, things that are not, to reduce to nothing things that are, so that no one might boast in the presence of God.*

1 Corinthians 1.26-29

Invite a response to the reading:

- What meaning does the reading have for today?

- Name people in the world today, including Britain and your local area, to whom Paul could have written those words.

4

Closing activity: Wanted! A Saint! *(15 minutes)*

The Church today needs saints, so advertise for one! Acting in groups of three or four, devise an advertising poster to encourage potential saints to contact you. Page 7 offers a pro-forma for the advert. Beneath the picture write a brief description of the experience, abilities, gender, qualities and age of the person required.

Alternatively, invite each group member to write down one quality expected in a saint and, taking turns, read it out and lay the paper where all can see it.

Look ahead to Session 2

- If the stories have not been taped locally, forewarn the people who will read the stories.

- There are also five short paragraphs to be read from the Bible.

- In order to continue the thinking begun in this session, suggest that the members of the group read the section *Saints in some of the different traditions* in **Appendix Two**.

Closing prayer *(10 minutes)*

Reflection

With the advertising poster(s) or slips of paper clearly visible, invite the members of the group to reflect silently on how they would themselves respond to the challenge of the advertisement or the expected qualities.

Prayer

After the silence, offer to God all that has been said and done. Then say:

> O God in whom all things live,
> you invite us to seek you
> and are always ready to be found:
> > to know you is life,
> > to serve you is freedom,
> > to praise you is our soul's delight.
> We bless you and we adore you,
> we worship you and we magnify you,
> we give thanks to you for your great glory
> through Jesus Christ our friend and Saviour. Amen.

Edinburgh

Belfast

Dublin

Cardiff

London

WANTED

Saints

There are several vacancies for saints to work in our area. Applications should be made to your local church as soon as possible.

Qualifications required

....

....

....

....

....

....

Session 2

Called to be saints: In every place

Aim

To explore how where people live affects the way they respond to the biblical call to be saints.

To achieve the aim:

- a prayer and a Bible reading celebrate the variety of places in which we see God acting;

- then our own imagination and the experience of others helps us to explore how 'where we live' affects 'how we serve';

- from Bible extracts we see how Jesus responded to 'place' in his mission;

- a prayer of commitment concludes the session.

Preparation before this session

- Prepare the plain postcards for the **Opening activity**.

- Four **Stories of saints and places** are given; decide which of them you will use.

- Either contact readers, or ensure you have the taped version if this has been prepared locally.

- Ask five people to read the biblical narrative under **Bible reflection**.

Opening worship *(10 minutes)*

Prayer

Gracious God, present in every place,
lovingly, you flung the gospel wide to land just where it would;
rejoiced as it took root, alike in barren desert and in lush green field;
with joy you see it take fresh life in city, town, and village life,
climb high-rise steps, and walk the corridors of power.
And we rejoice,
that Paul the Jew expressed the truth in Gentile terms,
and Hildegard could sing it in her cell;
that Julian nurtured it where sacred cloister met the noisy world;
and Francis saw its richness in his poverty;
that Lindisfarne became a Celtic home;
and Iona kept a rugged faith alive.

And can it still be true? Are we still alert?
Can our misted eyes see gospel roots still reaching out
to find a home, alike in praying church and alien world,
in city centre and suburban road,
in town hall, council chamber, factory floor,
and every place where people meet?

Grant, eternal God, that as once your Word became incarnate in living
flesh and breathing heart, present in synagogue and temple, Nazareth
home and lakeside conversation, manger bed and lonely cross, so we may
have eyes to see you in our present time and know you where we live.

© Donald Hilton, used with permission

Bible reading

Briefly introduce the reading by reminding the group that Paul wrote this
letter from prison, but that far from feeling depressed by this, he saw it as a
place where Christ gave him and others opportunities for witness they could
not otherwise have had.

*I want you to know, beloved, that what has happened to me has actually
helped to spread the gospel, so that it has become known throughout the
whole imperial guard and to everyone else that my imprisonment is for
Christ; and most of the brothers and sisters, having been made confident
in the Lord by my imprisonment, dare to speak the word with greater
boldness and without fear.*

Philippians 1.12-14

9

Opening activity *(20 minutes)*

Prepare six pieces of card. On one side of each card write one of the locations given below:

- a vibrant, busy city centre
- a village with no shop, post office or bank and one sparsely attended church
- a top-floor flat in a high-rise block
- a convent or monastery
- a prosperous suburb
- a long-term hospital bed

Place the cards upside down on a table so that the writing cannot be seen and ask each member of the group to take one. In large groups not everyone may be able to take part; some may have to observe in order to limit the time required. After reflecting on the situation described, invite those with cards to respond to the following questions:

- What changes would your new location make on your present life?
- What do you think is the best it would bring out of you?
- What do you think is the worst it would bring out in you?
- How do you think it might affect your faith?

Group leaders will know whether the participants would feel more comfortable speaking on their own or through a conversation with the leader. Remember throughout that the aim of the activity is to discover what effect the place where we live has on our lifestyle, attitudes, and Christian responsibility.

Stories of saints and places *(30 minutes)*

Four stories are given to illustrate how our surroundings can affect our calling to be saints. Use as many of them as possible, but if time is short, read some in full, and summarize the others.

1. *In the desert: Antony*

On his way to church one Sunday, Antony, a 20-year-old Egyptian, thought about the call of Jesus to 'Follow me', and the way the first disciples had taken

that literally and left all to follow Jesus. He remembered the story in the Acts of the Apostles (Acts 2.43-47) of how the early Christians had sold their possessions and given the money to the poor. He entered church as the Gospel was being read. The words underlined his earlier thoughts: 'If you would be perfect', he heard, 'go and sell what you have and give to the poor; and come follow me and you shall have treasure in heaven.'

Antony's life spanned the end of the third century and the beginning of the fourth. The church was no longer persecuted, the danger of martyrdom was over and as being a Christian now involved few risks, commitment to the faith began to decline. Those who wanted to live a more intense Christian life in full obedience to the gospel felt the urge to show a deeper commitment.

Living with this background Antony felt that what he had heard in church was a direct command from God. He gave away the three hundred acres of fertile land his father had left him, sold his other possessions, and gave all the

11

proceeds to the poor, keeping back only a little for the welfare of his sister. He then moved to live in solitude in the desert, devoting himself to prayer.

For twenty years he lived in the desert, trained himself in solitude and silence, and was rarely seen by others. But many people wanted to imitate his lifestyle and besieged his desert cell, even pulling off the wooden door. Antony emerged and, as described by Athanasius, the bishop of Alexandria at the time, they saw a man 'neither contracted as if by grief, nor relaxed by pleasure, nor possessed by laughter or dejection for he was not troubled when he beheld the crowd, nor overjoyed at being saluted by so many. He was altogether even as being guided by reason and abiding in a natural state.'

2. *In the city: George MacLeod*

In the 1920s the Church of Scotland's St Giles Cathedral in Edinburgh was surrounded by some of the worst housing in Scotland. Both poverty and tuberculosis were rife in the overcrowded slums. It was not unusual for twenty people to share the same water tap. Malnutrition made life a misery and, for many, drunkenness was the only way of escape. To this church George MacLeod came as assistant minister. His deep hope was to find ways of reaching and helping the young people in the area. His approach to young people was then unorthodox. 'I'll make a bargain with you', he told a group of lads lounging on the street corner. 'If you come to church next week I'll take you up the Cathedral tower and give you a fish and chip supper afterwards.'

When he moved to be minister of Govan Old Parish, Glasgow, in 1930, George MacLeod made it clear that his ministry was to be rooted in the local community. He moved from the manse and lived with other staff in a flat above the Pearce Institute set within the heart of an industrial community. The sounds that woke him each morning were of 'a thousand hammers, thundering on boilers of steam vessels which are to bridge the Atlantic or Pacific'.

He is best known for his rebuilding of the monastic living quarters of Iona Abbey and for creating a community on Iona with a wide outreach. The Community has become an educational focus for ministers and lay people; it remains a broad-based, pilgrim community for all who seek a new under-standing of what it means to be 'church'. MacLeod claimed that the real founder was Archie Campbell, a man who had heckled him at an open-air meeting. Some weeks after the meeting MacLeod was summoned to the hospital to see a man dying of starvation. A single man, he had left home because he was eating too much of the family's rations. It was Archie Campbell, who said he was bitter about the church not because it was preaching falsehood, but because it was preaching the truth, yet did not mean what it said. The story summarizes MacLeod's conviction that the Church has a powerful message which is often denied by the life and practice of the messenger.

3. In the valley: John Thomas Job

As the nineteenth century moved to its close, Lord Penrhyn was one of the most powerful owners in the North Wales slate-quarrying industry. Welsh slate was exported all over the world and from the middle of the century had been intensely profitable for its owners and shareholders. From his magnificent mock medieval castle near Bangor, Lord Penrhyn controlled the massive quarries up the Ogwen Valley in Bethesda. By the standards of his time *Yr Hen Lord* (The Old Lord), as he was called, was a fairly decent employer but when he died, his son, George Sholto Douglas, succeeded him and proved to be a much harder man. Draconian changes to working conditions eventually led to the longest strike in British industrial history. Beginning in November 1900 it lasted for three years.

Into the resulting despair, bitterness, and starvation came the Welsh Calvinistic Methodist minister John Thomas Job. He and fellow ministers organized collections throughout Britain and provided soup kitchens to support the strikers and their families who had nowhere else to turn for help.

Almost as destructive as the physical suffering was the personal animosity that sprang up. Some workers refused to strike or drifted back to the quarries as the months dragged on. *'Bradwyr'*, they were called – traitors! Members within the same family were divided. Troops were sent into Bethesda to quell the disorder which sprang out of the desperation of the miners and their families.

It was the Church that emerged as the reconciler, and J. T. Job as the peacemaker. Preacher and writer, he saw the wounds of the people, and agony of their plight. He pleaded: 'None but the Spirit can thoroughly heal our wounds.' Later, he wrote: 'Old bad feelings and old contentions are already vanishing before the breath of the Eternal Love.'

When the great revival of 1904/5 reached the town in the aftermath of the strike, J. T. Job was moved to write: 'Thanks be to God, forever, for remembering poor Bethesda.' Many were those who gave thanks to God for giving them the Methodist minister.

Information drawn from *Voices of the Welsh Revival*, Bridgend (Evangelical Press of Wales, 1995)

4. *In prison: John McCarthy*

The following is an account of an experience of John McCarthy while imprisoned in Beirut. After two months of solitary imprisonment he feared that he would not cope:

> One morning these fears became unbearable. I stood in the cell sinking into despair. I felt that I was literally sinking, being sucked down into a whirlpool. I was on my knees, gasping for air, drowning in hopelessness and helplessness. I thought that I was passing out. I could only think of one thing to say – 'Help me please, oh God, help me.' The next instant I was standing up, surrounded by a warm bright light. I was dancing, full of joy. In the space of a minute, despair had vanished, replaced by boundless optimism.
>
> What had happened? I had never had any great faith, despite a Church of England upbringing. But I felt that I had to give thanks. But to what? Unsure of the nature of the experience, I felt most comfortable acknowledging the Good Spirit which seemed to have rescued me.
>
> It gave me great strength to carry on and, more importantly, a huge renewal of hope – I was going to survive. Throughout my captivity, I would take comfort from this experience, drawing on it whenever optimism and determination flagged.
>
> From *Some Other Rainbow* by John McCarthy and Jill Morrell

Discussion

- How did 'place' affect the people in these stories?

- What do the stories tell us about the spiritual life of the people involved?

- What do we learn about God from these stories?

- Do you more readily identify with any one of the characters? If so, why?

Bible reflection *(10 minutes)*

Invite five people to read the following abridged version of Mark 1.16-39 as a continuous narrative. Tell the group that the readings will not be followed by discussion. They are invited simply to listen and note how, as the place changes, so Jesus responds to the new opportunity it provides.

The workplace – a place of challenge

As Jesus passed along the Sea of Galilee, he saw Simon and his brother Andrew casting a net into the lake – for they were fishermen. And Jesus said to them, 'Follow me and I will make you fish for people.' And immediately they left their nets and followed him.

The synagogue – a place for teaching and spiritual renewal

They went to Capernaum; and when the sabbath came, he entered the synagogue and taught. Just then there was in their synagogue a man with an unclean spirit, and he cried out, 'What have you to do with us, Jesus of Nazareth? Have you come to destroy us? I know who you are, the Holy One of God.' But Jesus rebuked him, saying, 'Be silent, and come out of him!' And the unclean spirit, throwing him into convulsions and crying with a loud voice, came out of him.

Home – a place for care

As soon as they left the synagogue, they entered the house of Simon and Andrew, with James and John. Now Simon's mother-in-law was in bed with a fever, and they told him about her at once. He came and took her by the hand and lifted her up. Then the fever left her, and she began to serve them. The whole city was gathered around the door. And he cured many who were sick with various diseases.

Solitude – a place for prayer

In the morning while it was still very dark, he got up and went out to a deserted place, and there he prayed.

Travelling – places for mission

Simon and his companions hunted for him. When they found him, they said to him, 'Everyone is searching for you.' He answered, 'Let us go on to the neighbouring towns, so that I may proclaim the message there also; for that is what I came out to do.'

Where we are *(15 minutes)*

Think about the location of the churches represented in the group.

- What are the needs and opportunities of the areas around the churches?
- What is the specific task of mission and ministry those places suggest?
- What work is crying out to be done?

Look ahead to Session 3

- Can others help with the photocopying of next week's activity sheet? (see pages 24–5) (Extra copies will be needed if the group is to divide.)
- Are you going to add other saints' names and profiles?
- Will you need help with the story-telling?

Closing worship (*5 minutes*)

Conclude the session with the following prayer.

Leader	We are called to be saints in (*name your town/village/etc.*)
	Silence
Leader	Lord, in the place where you have set us
All	**Help us truly to be your people**
Leader	We are called to be saints in our workplace
	Silence
Leader	Lord, in the place where you have set us
All	**Help us truly to be your people**
Leader:	We are called to be saints in our leisure
	Silence
Leader	Lord, in the place where you have set us
All	**Help us truly to be your people**
Leader	We are called to be saints in our churches
	Silence
Leader	Lord, in the place where you have set us
All	**Help us truly to be your people**
Leader	We are called to be saints in our relationships with each other
	Silence
Leader	Lord, in the place where you have set us
All	**Help us truly to be your people**
Leader	We are called to be saints in our homes
	Silence
Leader	Lord, in the place where you have set us
All	**Help us truly to be your people**

Session 3

Called to be saints: At the right time

Aim

To identify how God speaks and acts through individuals and communities, both throughout history and in our own time, always meeting the needs of the moment.

To achieve the aim:

- after worship we create a simple time-line to remind the group when some well-known saints lived – their profiles help us to see how they responded to the needs of their time;

- a Bible story shows the reaction between Jesus and a woman on one specific day, and more recent stories reveal the timely response of two Christians to their particular circumstances;

- the widespread response to the death of two well-known women in the same week makes us ask if the present-day use of words like 'saint' and 'icon' is leading to confusion;

- a prayer concludes the session.

Preparation before this session

- For the **Time-line of saints activity**, photocopy the activity sheet (see pages 24–5); if possible, use the photocopier to enlarge the sheet. Very large groups may wish to divide into smaller groups, each of which would then need a copy of the activity sheet.

- From the photocopy, cut out the individual names of the saints, and the short descriptive profiles. Note that spaces have been left so that additional saints and their profiles can be added by the group.

- Familiarize yourself with the saints and their profiles.

- Provide a piece of string or wool, approximately three to four metres long, for each group, to act as the time-line.

Introduction and opening worship *(10 minutes)*

Introduce the session by reading the aim.

In every age, and often in response to specific cultural, political, and social circumstances, people have emerged to challenge and inspire their own generation. By the grace of God they have been 'people for their own time' although their influence has also been felt in later ages. Allow a brief period of silence for reflection to prepare mind and heart. Then offer the prayer.

> **All** **The Spirit of God is upon me,**
> **who has anointed me to bring good news to those who are poor,**
> **who has sent me to proclaim release to those who are captive,**
> **and recovery of sight to those who are blind,**
> **to let those who are oppressed go free,**
> **to proclaim the year of God's favour.**

Opening activity: A time-line of saints *(20 minutes)*

To demonstrate how saints have emerged at the 'right' time throughout history, invite the group (or each smaller group where required) to lay their string or wool on the floor in a straight line to mark a time-line from 2000 BC to AD 2000. It might help to mark the centre point as '0'.

First, give the group(s) the names of the saints you have cut from your photocopy of pages 24–5 and ask them to lay them on approximately the right historical place on the time-line. When that is complete invite the group to add the profiles to the time-line, matching each profile to the right person. Let the group add other saints' names, if they wish.

When the task is completed, choose three or four of the saints. Consider them one by one, and create discussion around the following questions.

- How did the saint respond to the circumstances of his/her time?
- In what ways were new communities formed?
- How is God seen in the circumstances of their lives?
- What lessons can we learn from this for today?

Bible reading and discussion: A foreign woman challenges Jesus *(20 minutes)*

Despite being both a woman and a Gentile, both of which facts would make a direct approach to Jesus unusual, if not scandalous, this Syrophoenician seized the moment to plead for her daughter.

From there he set out and went away to the region of Tyre. He entered a house and did not want anyone to know he was there. Yet he could not escape notice, but a woman whose little daughter had an unclean spirit immediately heard about him, and she came and bowed down at his feet. Now the woman was a Gentile, of Syrophoenician origin. She begged him to cast the demon out of her daughter. He said to her, 'Let the children be fed first, for it is not fair to take the children's food and throw it to the dogs.' But she answered him, 'Sir, even the dogs under the table eat the children's crumbs.' Then he said to her, 'For saying that, you may go – the demon has left your daughter.' So she went home, found the child lying on the bed, and the demon gone.

Mark 7.24-30

- What qualities did the woman show?
- In what way was the encounter a challenge to Jesus?

Saints in our time (20 *minutes*)

1. *In the face of betrayal: Enoe*

Enoe writes of the time during the civil war in El Salvador (c. 1977–1992)

When I was about twelve I began to give catechism classes in the canton where we lived. I liked religion and singing from the book that the sisters here know well. Later, people began to organize because where we lived there was a lot of poverty.

All the people met in the main church and read from the Bible in groups and discussed and commented on the readings. It was all based on real life, on the life we were living then; the poverty and oppression. We had always been told that the poor were poor and we would get our reward in the next life. I woke up and said, 'Yes, but there is a way of changing this.' We could go ahead and do something.

The security forces began to persecute people who read the Bible. We began to work as women although it was not easy to take women from all the tasks in the house, looking after the children, everything in the house. It is difficult, it costs, it is complicated. But we were strong during the war although they bombed and shelled us, we went ahead and did a lot to change the situation. The struggle has gone on for centuries, but if we don't claim our rights and ask that we be respected as human beings, nothing will happen. We have to face up to this situation. Together.

As we left the meeting, we saw a woman sitting on the pavement. She got up and moved off as we looked at her. It was explained that she had 'put the finger' on several people – betrayed them to the security forces – who were later murdered, but the other women bore her no malice. They have forgiven her. They know she did it for money, because she was poor.

Adapted from Life out of Death: the feminine spirit in El Salvador

2. *In the face of adversity: Leonard Bird (1910–1996)*

Even before he became a Quaker in 1939, Leonard Bird was committed to the quest for peace. By word and action it was clear that he was guided by the grace of God to be valiant for peace throughout his adult life. He held an absolute opposition to war and all aspects of human conflict. He was imprisoned on three occasions for his pacifist beliefs. He would brook no compromise to his beliefs and his obduracy led him, on occasions, to being out of fellowship with Friends who could not hold wholeheartedly to his ideas and activities.

Visiting the Soviet Union several times, he was keen to foster contacts between people there and in Britain. He promoted the tripartite work-camps of the Soviet, American, and British young people, believing that campaigns for disarmament alone were not the key to a peaceful future; work must be done at the point where the desire for conflict arose.

Brought up as a child in Huddersfield during the First World War, Leonard saw and experienced poverty and deprivation in his formative years. He spoke out and acted in support of all who were deprived of dignified conditions of living. As well as his professional work as a solicitor – where he would sometimes accept work for needy people without prospect of a fee – he also served as a Quaker prison visitor.

A sparkling, dynamic driving force, he spoke powerfully of the strength and support of the divine Spirit working within and throughout his life. He walked cheerfully over the world, striving to answer that of God in everyone; an example to all who would adventure to establish a peaceable kingdom for all peoples and nations.

Adapted from Testimonies – Pickering and Hull Monthly Quaker Meeting (1997)

- What saintly qualities, if any, do these two stories identify?
- In what ways can saints bring problems with them?
- How did the time in which the people lived affect their beliefs and lifestyle?
- How did they respond to the needs of their communities?

Icons, idols, and saints *(15 minutes)*

'Icons' and 'idols' are words with precise and specialist meanings, but they are also popular titles. We have 'pop idols'. We describe people of renown as 'icons'. 'Saint' is used both for the figure on the stained-glass window and the humble, self-effacing person who lives up the street. This course is widening our view of 'saints', but are there any guidelines or restrictions to our use of the word?

The Churches for whom icons are a part of their spirituality and worship regard them as an expression in visual form of the central doctrines of the faith, and they are therefore created as an act of loving religious devotion. They become 'windows onto the divine'.

'Idol' has normally been understood as an image of a false god, although the Jewish tradition rejects images even of the true God. In the New Testament, idolatry refers also to giving priority to interests other than God, a line followed by Christian expositors, including Luther in his Catechism. (Information drawn from *A New Dictionary of Christian Theology*, SCM Press, 1969)

In the early days of the Christian Church, saints were recognized through popular acclaim. Many were from noble and royal families. Even in their lifetime, people would travel for days to meet them. There was an expectation of miracles and great excitement (hysteria?) among the crowds. It was not unlike the media idols of our own day.

Two well-known women died in the same week in 1997: Diana, Princess of Wales and Mother Teresa of Calcutta. They had met each other in their lifetimes. Both received great admiration and popular acclaim. They were 'icons', and popular opinion suggested that both were 'saints'. Who can forget the slightly bowed figure in white, bending over the dying in Calcutta? Who can forget the images of Diana walking through the minefields or cuddling children without limbs? The death of Diana led to a great popular outpouring of emotion with candles, flowers and songs; a shrine was built in her memory on an island in the middle of the lake at Althorp. Equally dramatic scenes took place in India as vast crowds marked Mother Teresa's death.

Both women received criticism in their lifetime: Diana for suggested manipulation, Teresa for a perceived autocratic attitude about her style of work.

- Why, in their different ways, were these two women inspiring?

- What do the responses to the deaths of Mother Teresa and Princess Diana tell us about, firstly, the society we live in, and secondly, ourselves?

Look ahead to Session 4

- Invite the group members to bring a photograph or picture of someone who has been an inspiration to them in their faith journey.

- Let the group decide whether to use candles (or tea-lights), pebbles or flowers. Would group members like to bring their own pebbles or flowers if these are chosen?

- Session 4 requires several stories to be read. Decide how the group will do this.

Closing prayer *(5 minutes)*

Encourage a few moments of quiet reflection on the session, inviting members of the group to think about their opportunities to be saints. How can they respond to the opportunities?

Prayer

Leader   For all the saints
who went before us,
who have spoken to our hearts
and have touched us with your fire,

All   **we praise you, O God.**

Leader   For all the saints
who live beside us,
whose weaknesses and strengths
are woven with our own,

All   **we praise you, O God.**

Leader   For all the saints
who live beyond us,
who challenge us
to change the world with them,

All   **we praise you, O God.**

From *Bread of Tomorrow*, ed. Janet Morley

TIME-LINE OF SAINTS ACTIVITY SHEET

Mother Teresa 1910-1997	**George MacLeod** 1895-1991
Janet Lacey 1903-1988	**Mother Julian of Norwich** c.1342-c.1420
Hilda of Whitby 614-680	**Martin Luther** 1483-1546
Miriam c.1250 BC	**John the Baptist** early first century
King David c.1000 BC	**Amos** c.760 BC
Name your own choice of a saint	*Name your own choice of a saint*

I was born in Sunderland. First a youth worker, I later worked with refugees in Germany after World War 2. Later, while I was working for the British Council of Churches, I helped set up Christian Aid. I was the first woman to preach in St Paul's Cathedral, London.	Although an officer in the Argyll and Sutherland Highlanders (1914), I later became a pacifist. I spearheaded the rebuilding programme on Iona; young ministers came to work there as craftsmen and to prepare for mission in industrial areas. I used the symbol of the Wild Goose for the Iona Community which is now well known for its music and prayers.
I was born into a noble family from Northumbria and founded an abbey based on justice and equality. I worked hard to reconcile the Celtic and Roman traditions and bring about reconciliation in troubled times.	People around me were dying of the greatest scourge of my time, the Black Death. I lived alone in my cell, with a window facing out to the world. I was the first woman known to have written a book in English.

I was born in Skopje. My parents were Albanian. I left my convent in Calcutta to work among the dying in disease-ridden slums. I was awarded a Nobel Prize for my world-wide mission among the poor and abandoned.

Living in the eighth century BC, I was a shepherd in Tekoa, Judah at a time when, although Israel was prosperous and the sanctuaries filled with people, worship was insincere. Travelling north I spoke strongly against injustice and superficial religion. I warned that the hoped-for 'day of the Lord' would be a day of judgement, not easy privilege.

I lived during a time when Egypt ruled over the Hebrews. My mother placed my baby brother in a basket and cast him afloat upon a river in the hope he would be saved. I kept watch and when he was found by an Egyptian princess, I suggested my mother to her as a wet nurse.

I was an Augustinian friar and a professor of theology in Germany. I caused a controversy by speaking out against abuses in the Church of my day. I was excommunicated in 1521 and attributed with causing the Reformation.

I am variously described as a shepherd boy, a musician, a rebel fighter and a giant killer. I had a close friend called Jonathan. My kingly reign became a symbol of a 'golden age' for my country.

I was born in the first century to Elizabeth and Zechariah. I became a wandering preacher in the Jordan desert. I was renowned for being outspoken, denouncing the hypocrisy of the religious leaders.

Profile of your own choice of saint

Profile of your own choice of saint

Session 4

Called to be saints: The hidden revealed

Aim

To commemorate those saints who, though largely unknown, have faithfully played their part and inspired others in faith and service.

To achieve the aim:

- stage by stage we reveal 'unknown saints' from the Bible, more recent times, and our own experience;

- we hear the stories of this 'cloud of witnesses', who have glorified God;

- without detailed discussion, but by silent reflection and simple action, we commemorate each one of them, and what they represent.

Preparation for this session

- Invite the group to bring a photograph or picture of someone who has been an inspiration to them. This is for the **Saints at hand** activity. They may be personal friends, or saints honoured in one Christian tradition but unknown to others.

- You will need candles (or tea-lights), or pebbles, or flowers (and a vase), depending on the form of commemoration you choose in **Saints revealed**, and in **Saints at hand**.

- Five stories of 'hidden saints' are given which is probably more than you can use. Decide which to use, how to present them, and which member of the group will lead each act of commemoration.

- If you use music during the acts of commemoration ensure that a Taizé or other chant (recorded or sung by the group) is available.

Opening worship *(5 minutes)*

Prayer

> Glory to you, O God,
> for Christian saints
> whose ancient voices still resound with truth,
> whose names are well-remembered in our time,
> to challenge and inspire our present lives.
>
> Glory to you, O God,
> for Christian saints
> whose names have missed the pages of our history,
> who lived their lives off-stage;
> known but to the few,
> yet who, in this small circle, that modest place,
> were faithful to their Lord;
> saw well their task, and well fulfilled it,
> who lived unknown, and died forgotten
> but yet,
> by grace and love, integrity and care,
> lived out the gospel life
> and sent a silent voice down through the years;
> a soundless testimony.
>
> And gave glory to you, O God.

Opening activity *(10 minutes)*

Introduce this session by suggesting that it requires careful thought from the group. It is difficult to commemorate and give thanks for 'unknown saints' – we do not know them! Yet countless less well-known people have served God faithfully, and some of them have triggered faith and action in others.

Create a display of the pictures or photographs that group members have brought to the session. They could be attached to a large sheet of card or laid flat on a table-top, but ensure that they are readily visible throughout the session, symbolizing the aim.

Bible study: The man behind Paul (15 minutes)

Paul (originally called Saul) was a remarkable Christian missionary. He founded many churches during three major missionary journeys, and wrote significant letters to them that have provided a theological foundation for the gospel. Alongside the Gospels his letters have sustained Christians in every generation since. He died a martyr's death in Rome. Standing centre stage in early Christian history, his stature has never diminished.

But would he have made that contribution without the faith and action of another man – Stephen – who, though still honoured, receives much less notice than Paul.

Stephen played a major part in the mission of the Church but his eloquent and persuasive preaching invited opposition from the Jewish authorities. The Acts of the Apostles includes the message Stephen daringly preached to show that the authorities had always resisted God's purpose – and had done so again in crucifying Jesus. He concludes:

> *Which of the prophets did your ancestors not persecute? They killed those who foretold the coming of the Righteous One, and now you have become his betrayers and murderers.*

> *When they heard these things, they became enraged and ground their teeth at Stephen. But filled with the Holy Spirit, he gazed into heaven and saw the glory of God and Jesus standing at the right hand of God. 'Look,' he said, 'I see the heavens opened and the Son of Man standing at the right hand of God!' But they covered their ears, and with a loud shout all rushed together against him. Then they dragged him out of the city and began to stone him; and the witnesses laid their coats at the feet of a young man named Saul. While they were stoning Stephen, he prayed, 'Lord Jesus, receive my spirit.' Then he knelt down and cried out in a loud voice, 'Lord, do not hold this sin against them.' When he had said this, he died. And Saul approved of their killing him.*

> Acts 7.52, 54 – 8.1

- What effect might Stephen's death and amazing forgiveness have had on Paul?

- What role might Stephen have played in Paul's conversion?

- Have some 'hidden saints' had a knock-on effect on others, the unknown saint triggering action in the well-known saint? Think of others apart from Paul and Stephen.

Saints revealed *(40 minutes)*

Five stories follow, each of which reveals an 'unknown' saint. It is unlikely that you will be able to use all five in the time available. In advance of the session, read each one carefully and decide which of them will best bring out the theme of the session for your group. Invite each of several people to read one of them (or use the taped version if it has been produced). Do not discuss the stories; let them, and the people within them, speak for themselves. Follow each one with a quiet act of commemoration (more detailed suggestions are given after each story). A Taizé or other chant could also be used.

Suggested form of commemoration after each story

- Silence for reflection.

- Invite the whole group to stand, as one member of the group lights a candle (or tea-light), or places a pebble on the table to form a pile of pebbles, or places a flower in a vase, and says:

- 'With this candle/pebble/flower we honour (*the name of the unknown saint*) etc.'

1. *The woman behind Martin Luther King*

On Thursday 1 December 1955 a 42-year-old woman, Rosa Parks, was arrested in Montgomery, Alabama, USA. She was returning home after her day's work as a tailor's assistant. She took her seat on the bus and soon the bus was full. A white man was left standing. The bus driver ordered Rosa and three other African-American passengers to move because under the city ordinance no black person was allowed to sit parallel with a white passenger. It was not unknown for a pregnant black woman to be forced to stand so that a white teenager could sit.

The other three reluctantly moved but Rosa Parks did not. Three times the bus driver, J. F. Blake, told her to move and she simply said: 'No'. Warned that she would be arrested, Mrs Parks told him to go right ahead. Blake left the bus and called the police. Rosa Parks was detained.

Because of the widespread resentment of the rules, Rosa Parks' action could have sparked a violent reaction by black people against whites, but a group of black ministers united with the City Women's Political Council to propose a boycott of all city buses on 5 December. As 70 per cent of the travelling public was black the action was highly successful.

The situation worsened when it became known that Rosa Parks had been found guilty and fined $10. Five thousand people met in the Holt Street Baptist Chapel and decided to form a committee to be known as the 'Montgomery Improvement Association' which would work for the desegregation of the city public transport. The boycott continued for 382 days despite police persecution and the hardship of walking everywhere for such a long period. Naturally the Association had to have a president. They elected the then little-known minister of Dexter Avenue Baptist Church. His name was Dr Martin Luther King.

The reason for Rosa Parks' act of defiance has been interpreted in different ways. She has been seen as an elderly woman who refused to obey the driver because she was tired and 'my feet hurt'. Others say that, although tired after a day's work, she did not think of herself as old at 42. She refused to give up her seat because she was tired of giving in.

The significance of her action was profound. Martin Luther King organized an effective campaign of peaceful resistance. On one occasion thousands of people staged a massive sit-down in Washington. One commentator puts it succinctly: Martin Luther King would never have sat down in the middle of a Washington street if Rosa Parks had not refused to stand up on the Montgomery bus.

Act of commemoration:

- Silence for reflection.

- The group standing, one member lights a candle or places a pebble or flower and says: 'With this candle/pebble/flower we honour Rosa Parks and all who work for justice.'

2. *The man behind the headlines*

On Sunday 8 November 1987, as people gathered around the Enniskillen cenotaph, an IRA bomb exploded. Eleven people died; there was extensive damage. Gordon Wilson and his daughter Marie were buried in the rubble. As they held hands, Marie, a nurse, died. That same evening Gordon Wilson gave a spontaneous and memorable interview to a BBC reporter. Some criticized him for what he said; others were amazed at the spirit of reconciliation he expressed. Later, he wrote:

> I like to think that it was the real Gordon Wilson who spoke to the BBC's reporter, Mike Gaston, on the evening of the bomb, when I said, 'I have lost my daughter and we shall miss her. But I bear no ill will. I bear no grudge. Dirty sort of talk is not going to bring her back … She was a pet. She's dead. She's in heaven and we'll meet again. Don't ask me please, for a purpose. I don't have a purpose. I don't have an answer. But I know there has to be a plan. If I didn't think that, I would commit suicide. It's part of a greater plan, and God is good. And we shall meet again.'
>
> I did not use the word 'forgive' in that broadcast, nor in any later one, but people understood that my words were about forgiveness. Our Lord taught us to pray, 'Forgive us our sins, as we forgive those who sin against us.' We ask God to forgive us, but we are always subjected to his condition that we must forgive others. God's forgiveness is ultimate, ours is the forgiveness of man to man. To me, the two become one. It's as simple as that. My words were not intended as a statement of theology or of righteousness, rather they were from the heart, and they expressed how I felt at the time, and as I still do.

From *Marie, a story from Enniskillen*, by Gordon Wilson with Alf McCreary

Act of commemoration:

- Silence for reflection.

- The group standing, one member lights a candle or places a pebble or flower and says: 'With this candle/pebble/flower we honour Gordon Wilson and all who, having been wronged, have forgiven.'

3. *The woman behind Christian Aid: Janet Lacey*

'I was shattered,' she said, 'and drama did not seem to matter any more.' Janet Lacey was a writer and dramatist. She had produced her first play at the age of thirteen, working with 25 children in her local Wesleyan chapel in Sunderland. It was clear that her talents lay in acting and producing plays. She studied at a technical school near Durham and had drama and elocution lessons in a small, private drama school. She was 'shattered' when she saw cruel poverty among Durham miners in the strike of 1926.

She had never forgotten an experience when out for a walk one cold day in 1915. Twelve years old, she was pushed back from the pavement edge by policemen. A long procession of vehicles passed by full of wounded men. They were filthy and packed like sardines. The air was filled with their groans and the stench of festering wounds. She was rushed away from the awful scene but heard afterwards of the townspeople's realization that a new kind of war was being fought and life would never be the same again.

With such an experience living in her memory, the later experience of the poverty of striking Durham miners gave her life a new direction. She became a trainee at the Kendal YWCA, in order to become a youth leader. She was, in fact, still able to use her skills and training in drama. She worked for many years with youth clubs, using acting to promote membership of the clubs. Later, her commitment to deprived and uprooted people led her to Dagenham in Essex where 200,000 workers had been resettled from the East End of London.

She became painfully aware of the quarter of a million post-war refugees who had settled in Britain and so served the Inter-Church Aid and Refugee Service of the British Council of Churches. Out of this grew Christian Aid, to which she was appointed as Director from 1952 to 1968. Her abilities were organizational; her motivation was, once again, to stand alongside the deprived and lost. Although she wrote many books and pamphlets about Christian Aid, she rarely described her own part in its development. Only a diminishing minority would now recall her name.

When asked in a radio interview if she had ever felt called by God to do compassionate work for those in need, she said, 'No, not that I am aware of.' For some the instinct to service needs no Damascus road; God has already spoken through human experience.

Act of commemoration:

- Silence for reflection.
- The group standing, one member lights a candle or places a pebble or flower and says: 'With this candle/pebble/flower we honour Janet Lacey and all communities that foster compassion.'

4. The community behind the parents behind the tragedy: Wendover Free Church

The last time his parents, Ursula and Colin, saw their youngest son alive was in June 1999. Eighteen-year-old Jonathan Coles said goodbye and went off, first to sit an A level exam and then to a friend's eighteenth-birthday celebration.

The celebrations ended at a Milton Keynes nightclub. Whilst waiting for a taxi to take them home, the group of friends were set upon. In the ensuing chase, Jonny was separated from the others. He was beaten and robbed of his bank card and lost his glasses. Finding no money in his account, a group of four young men abducted Jonny as he sought help. He was driven off, and despite saying he couldn't swim, he was thrown off a high bridge at a local beauty spot and drowned. It was six days before his body was found.

In those nightmare days of waiting for news, school friends and their parents joined the search. Wendover Free Church (Baptist/URC LEP), where Ursula and Colin are members, accepted that they must not phone, but leave the line open for officialdom. People felt helpless, but could and did pray, with the network spreading out beyond the immediate community. Ursula and Colin sensed they were being held as in a warm, comfy bath-towel.

The evening Jonny was found, the family needed privacy. Others needed a place to come. The Christian Centre was opened and for three hours it was candles and tears, a mix of generations, of the churchy and the unchurched, and queues to write in books of condolence, a time and place to be together in grief.

February 2000 saw three convicted of murder and the car-driver of man-slaughter. During the three-week trial, full details of the horrors faced by Jonny became public. Anger in the Wendover community was tangible. With a quiet dignity that impressed all, including the police, Ursula and Colin Coles sought justice not revenge. While the media clamoured for interviews, the church community sought not to intrude, but provided meals after long days in court. And prayer continued for the Coles family and for those convicted and their families. For as Ursula said, 'All these boys have caused their families extreme pain. The whole thing is very, very sad. I just hope they have had some loving family and friends to help each other.'

Written by Ruth Bottoms, Minister, Wendover Free Church, in consultation with Colin and Ursula Coles

Act of commemoration:

- Silence for reflection.
- The group standing, one member lights a candle or places a pebble or flower and says: 'With this candle/pebble/flower we honour the Coles family and all upholding and supportive communities.'

5. *The woman behind the praise: Ruth Hughes*

Ann Griffiths was born in 1776 and died in 1805. Although dying in child-birth at the age of 29, in her brief life she composed hymns and spiritual monologues in the Welsh language that have sustained Welsh-speaking congregations to this day, and now, belatedly, have become widely known and used in translation.

The known details of her short life are sparse. Some suggest that she led a rather wild life before her conversion but others say that there was nothing remarkable about her early years either in saintliness or vice. What is more likely is that, following the pattern of the time, her past errors were exaggerated to emphasize the genuine wonder of her conversion. Her Christian life began from the influence of the preaching of Calvinistic John Hughes of Pontrobert, Mid Wales, during the Methodist revival.

Y Ferch o Ddolwar Fach – the girl from Dolwar Fach – was the wife of a Welsh farmer. She composed her hymns as she went about her housework, or in the early morning quietness of her farmhouse in the hills of what we now know as North Powys. They carry the evangelical enthusiasm of revivalism and also reflect an older Celtic mystical tradition. Many of them celebrate the closeness of her relationship with Jesus Christ.

1. O! am fywyd a sancteiddio
   Sanctaidd enw pur fy Nuw,
   Ac ymostwng i'w ewyllys
   A'i lywodraeth tra fwy' byw;
   Byw gan addunedu a thalu,
   Dan ymnerthu yn y gras
   Sydd yng Nghrist yn drysoredig,
   I orchfygu y maes.

1. Let my life be spent in blessing
   Holy God's most blessed name.
   To his will my life submitting,
   All my life his rule proclaim.
   I would live beneath his promise
   And in strengthening of his grace;
   Live in Christ, who as the conqueror
   Won the victory in my place.

2. Daily would I sing the praises
   Of his blood 'til life shall end.
   I would rest beneath his shadow,
   Live and die beside my friend.
   I would love and bear the cross that
   My dear Husband bore for me.
   I would gaze upon his person;
   Praise my God eternally.

3. Here's the one who came as Brother
   Born to bear our grief and pain.
   One who's faithful, full of mercy,
   Worthy of the heart's acclaim.
   Seal of freedom, ailment's healer,
   Only road to Zion above:
   Cleansing fountain, great life-giver,
   Saving ark and God of love.

Translated by David Fox, this hymn can be sung to the tune *Prysgol*

But although Ann Griffiths and her hymns were 'hidden', except to Welsh-speaking congregations, until comparatively recently, she is not the hidden saint this story reveals. Unconvinced of the value of her hymns, Ann refused to commit them to writing and saw them only as an expression of her own spirituality, composed for her personal spiritual comfort. But this young farmer's wife had a maid, Ruth Hughes. Unusually for the time in which she lived, Ruth could read and write. As her mistress composed and sang, so Ruth memorized the words, and later wrote them down. Eventually, she preserved and treasured some seventy verses of hymns which would otherwise have been lost. We know little about Ruth Hughes except that her patience and commitment have given us these treasures of Welsh hymnody.

1. Rhyfedd, rhyfedd gan angylion,
   Rhyfeddod fawr yng ngolwg ffydd,
   Gweld rhoddwr bod, cynhaliwr helaeth
   A rheolwr pob beth sydd,
   Yn y preseb mewn cadachau
   Ac heb le i roi'i ben i lawr,
   Ac eto disglair lu'r gogoniant,
   Yn ei addoli ef yn awr.

   Diolch byth, a chanmil diolch,
   Diolch tra bo yno'i chwyth
   Am fod gwrthrych i'w addoli
   A thestun cân i bara byth;
   Yn fy natur wedi ei demtio
   Fel y gwacla' o ddynol ryw,
   Yn ddyn bach, yn wan, yn ddinerth,
   Yn anfeidrol wir a bywiol Dduw.

1. Wondrous, wondrous to the angels,
wondrous to the saints of old;
that the God who made and rules us
and the whole creation holds,
now lies swaddled in a manger,
born into our world of care,
yet a shining host in glory
bring him worship, bring him prayer.

2. Thousand, thousand thanks, and endless,
all my life shall sing the praise
of my God who for my worship
wondrous powers in manger lays.
Here in tempted human nature,
here – like weakest of our face,
here as helpless human infant,
here is God in power and grace.

Translated by David Fox, this hymn can be sung to the tune Esther

Act of commemoration:

- Silence for reflection.

- The group standing, one member lights a candle or places a pebble or flower and says: 'With this candle/pebble/flower we honour Ruth Hughes and all whose quiet work has provided rich resources for the worshipping community.'

Saints at hand *(15 minutes)*

Invite those group members whose pictures or photographs of inspiring people have been displayed, briefly to tell of their influence on their lives. As they conclude their short comment let them light a candle or place a pebble or flower and say: 'With this lighted candle/pebble/flower I honour the influence of (*name*).'

Look ahead to Session 5

- Ask each member of the group to search through newspapers (local and national) during the week and find one item of good news and one item of bad news, cut out the excerpts (preferably with pictures), and bring them to the next session.

- Note that a single candle is to be passed round the group; make sure it is in a stable candlestick or holder, that it will not drip wax, and that normal safety precautions are followed.

- Encourage the group members to read Ephesians 4 during the coming week.

Closing worship *(5 minutes)*

Bible reading

> *Since we are surrounded by so great a cloud of witnesses, let us lay aside every weight and the sin that clings so closely, and let us run with perseverance the race that is set before us, looking to Jesus the pioneer and perfecter of our faith, who for the sake of the joy that was set before him endured the cross, disregarding its shame, and has taken his seat at the right hand of the throne of God.*

Hebrews 12.1,2

Prayer

Use one of the following:

Either

Let us who have beheld the resurrection of Christ worship our holy Lord Jesus, who alone is without sin. We worship your cross, O Christ, praise and glorify your holy resurrection. For you are our God and we know none other besides you, and we call upon your Name. Come all ye faithful, let us worship Christ's holy resurrection for behold, through the Cross, joy has come to the entire world. We praise His resurrection and forever glorify the Lord. He endured the Cross for us, and by death destroyed death.

Jesus, having risen from the grave as he foretold, has given to us eternal life and his great mercy.

A Christian Resurrection Ode of the Orthodox Church

Or

Thanks be to thee, O Lord,
for saints thy Spirit stirred
in humble paths to live thy life and speak thy word.
Unnumbered they,
whose candles shine
to lead our footsteps after thine.

Lord God of truth and love,
'thy kingdom come' we pray;
give us thy grace to know thy truth and walk thy way:
that here on earth
thy will be done,
till saints in earth and heaven are one.

H. C. A. Gaunt

Session 5

Called to be saints: Equipped for tomorrow

Aim

To think about the world in which we live, and plan how to create communities of hope for today and for the future.

To achieve the aim:

- as a symbol of the five weeks' study, the Bible is set in a central position;
- we focus on Ephesians 4 to seek to understand how Christian individuals and communities can be equipped for future service;
- we consider the good and bad news in our daily newspapers, to remind us of the nature of the world we live in as we accept the challenge to our churches to become 'communities of hope';
- glimpses of such communities are given from the four nations of Britain and Ireland;
- in an act of commitment we close the week and the course, rejoicing in the constant leadership of Jesus Christ.

Preparation before this session

- You will need a Bible and an unlit candle on a central table. Note that when the candle is lit for the **Closing worship**, it will be passed from hand to hand around the group. Ensure that the candle is firmly held in a stable holder, and will not drip wax onto the carpet or floor.
- For the **Bible study: Equipping the saints** you will need two large sheets of paper. Head one sheet *Our Problems* and the other, *Our Solutions*. Marker pens are also needed. Make yourself familiar with the boxed sections within the Bible study. Alert a couple of other group members to look at these boxed sections so that the discussion flows quickly and can be kept within the timetable suggested.

> • For **What the papers say** the members of the group will need to have brought with them two cut-out excerpts from recent local or national newspapers, preferably with pictures. One cutting should reflect bad news and the other, good news. Take a few extra newspaper cuttings to the group for those who forget their own.

Opening worship *(5 minutes)*

Display an open Bible and an unlit candle on a central table.

Prayer

Gathered at God's table,
the saints enjoy heaven's food and wine;
those who once limped, walk tall and dance with David;
those who were silent, shout gladly with Miriam;
those who on earth were considered odd, old or ignorant
no longer bend under the weight of prejudice or casual labels.
All join hands, not for old lang syne, but to sing a new song:

As we gather, remind us of the saints of yesterday,
challenge us with the stories of the saints of today,
and call us to be the saints of tomorrow. Amen.

© WGRG Iona Community (adapted)

Bible study: Equipping the saints *(30 minutes)*

Introduction

Paul is traditionally regarded as the author of the Letter to the Ephesians. If so, his comments about the church were not casual; he knew the church and its circumstances well, having spent almost three years with the Christians there. His honest criticism and advice sprang from both realism and love.

The following Bible study method was first used in small Christian communities in Latin America and is now widely used across the world. It begins by asking what the passage meant to those who first heard it, and then encourages each person in the group to reflect and, if they wish, to comment on the relevance of the passage for their own situation and community.

Note that the study proceeds in five steps.

Step 1 *(5 minutes)*

Ask two people to read aloud alternate paragraphs from Ephesians 4. It should be read slowly and prayerfully, and be followed by a time of silence for everyone to consider what the passage is saying to them personally.

> *I therefore, the prisoner in the Lord, beg you to lead a life worthy of the calling to which you have been called, with all humility and gentleness, with patience, bearing with one another in love, making every effort to maintain the unity of the Spirit in the bond of peace. There is one body and one Spirit, just as you were called to the one hope of your calling, one Lord, one faith, one baptism, one God and Father of all, who is above all and through all and in all.*

> *But each of us was given grace according to the measure of Christ's gift. Therefore it is said, 'When he ascended on high he made captivity itself a captive; he gave gifts to his people.'*

> *The gifts he gave were that some would be apostles, some prophets, some evangelists, some pastors and teachers, to equip the saints for the work of ministry, for building up the body of Christ, until all of us come to the unity of the faith and of the knowledge of the Son of God, to maturity, to*

the measure of the full stature of Christ. We must no longer be children, tossed to and fro and blown about by every wind of doctrine, by people's trickery, by their craftiness in deceitful scheming. But speaking the truth in love, we must grow up in every way into him who is the head, into Christ, from whom the whole body, joined and knit together by every ligament with which it is equipped, as each part is working properly, promotes the body's growth in building itself up in love.

Now this I affirm and insist on in the Lord: you must no longer live as the Gentiles live, in the futility of their minds. They are darkened in their understanding, alienated from the life of God because of their ignorance and hardness of heart. They have lost all sensitivity and have abandoned themselves to licentiousness, greedy to practise every kind of impurity. That is not the way you learned Christ! For surely you have heard about him and were taught in him, as truth is in Jesus. You were taught to put away your former way of life, your old self, corrupt and deluded by its lusts, and to be renewed in the spirit of your minds, and to clothe yourselves with the new self, created according to the likeness of God in true righteousness and holiness.

So then, putting away falsehood, let all of us speak the truth to our neighbours, for we are members of one another. Be angry but do not sin; do not let the sun go down on your anger, and do not make room for the devil. Thieves must give up their stealing; rather let them labour and work honestly with their own hands, so as to have something to share with the needy. Let no evil talk come out of your mouths, but only what is useful for building up, as there is need, so that your words may give grace to those who hear. And do not grieve the Holy Spirit of God, with which you were marked with a seal for the day of redemption. Put away from you all bitterness and wrath and anger and wrangling and slander, together with all malice, and be kind to one another, tender-hearted, forgiving one another, as God in Christ has forgiven you.

Ephesians 4.1-8, 11-32

Step 2 *(10 minutes)*

The following boxed comments suggest some of the problems in Ephesus which Paul identified in his letter, and some of the advice he gave as a solution to the problems. Are these comments a fair analysis? Should further comments be added to either box? If so, write them in the spaces provided.

Alternatively, the suggested problems and solutions written in the boxes could be written up on two large sheets of paper for all to see and add to.

Problems in the Church at Ephesus

It was a divided church.

They failed to recognize the Spirit's gifts in each other.

They were clinging to the old life before they knew Christ, and ignoring the call to a new life.

They had forgotten the apostles' teaching.

Paul's Solution

Live up to your calling, not down to your former life.

Honour the church as the body of Christ.

Remember that there is only one Lord, one faith, and one baptism.

Be honest with each other, without getting angry.

Forgive each other! - Christ has forgiven you!

Step 3 (5 minutes)

Head a large sheet of paper '**Our Problems**', and invite people to suggest what they consider to be the biggest problems facing their churches today. Write their ideas on the sheet, and discuss the ideas.

Step 4 (10 minutes)

Head another large sheet of paper '**Our Solutions**', and invite people to suggest ways in which these problems could be tackled.

Discuss the ideas.

Step 5

Suggest that the members of the group read the Bible passage again at home.

Equipped for today

Life is changing rapidly. The society in which we live is very different from even a few years ago. To understand how to be saints in today's world, we must try to understand that changing world.

1. Changing rooms (5 minutes)

Briefly think about one room in a house, e.g. a kitchen or living room. Identify everything that would not have been in it 50 years ago. This activity is only a starter to stir the imagination; avoid going into detail about whether the changes are for the better or worse; just note the widespread and rapid change we have experienced.

2. What the papers say (20 minutes)

To look more deeply at the world in which we are now called to be saints, invite the group members, one by one, briefly to summarize their good news/bad news newspaper excerpts, showing the picture if there is one, and then place the excerpts on a table around the open Bible and the unlit candle.

Either in the full group, or using smaller buzz groups, reflect on two questions:

- How do we celebrate the good news?

- How do we confront, challenge, and transform the bad news?

Communities of hope *(15 minutes)*

Across the world, there are many groups of Christians and churches seeking to share their faith in ways which are relevant to the communities around them. The following four communities from around Britain and Ireland have been involved in 'Building Bridges of Hope', a CTBI project (see **Appendix One** for further details). The project involves learning with and from Christian communities across Europe about what it means to be a missionary church today.

Read these stories aloud, being alert to the signs of hope they suggest. The four examples are not offered as 'success stories'; indeed, they remain very fragile. However, having made themselves aware of the needs in their local community, the people involved are taking the initiative, as they live out their calling to be saints.

A story from Scotland

In Bellshill, Lanarkshire, two of the churches (Orbiston and St Andrew's Church of Scotland) joined forces with members of the wider community to find ways to respond to the needs of the area, which had been decimated by the steel closures of the early 90s. Out of their efforts a major new community centre has been developed in the church premises, catering for almost 2,000 people per week. There is a range of some 25 weekly activities – from worship to aerobics, from credit union to café – and the centre's users are from a few weeks old to people in their nineties. The entire initiative grew out of a small theology group of ten people. They asked: 'What does it mean to be the church in Bellshill today?'

A story from Ireland

In West Belfast, Northern Ireland, four community groups (Cornerstone, Curragh, Mid-Springfield Road Community Association and Springfield Road Methodist Church) came together to found Forthspring Community Centre, developed by and serving both Roman Catholic and Protestant communities. The Centre, opened in 1996, is built into the 'peace-line' which separates the loyalist and nationalist communities. In the face of ongoing sectarian violence and mistrust, Forthspring is open to all and is committed to addressing local community concerns and to creating healthy relationships across the Springfield Road.

45

A story from England

In Cambridge, Zion Baptist Church has found ways of relating to the needs of the community around it. Although a very small church – and by its own admission, very vulnerable – the church has a big heart for the local community. Situated in the heart of the city, its prayer has been 'may your kingdom come' rather than 'may your church grow'. Over the last five years nine major gospel projects have been developed, including a night shelter, a community transport scheme, a food bank and a football team! Throughout all the change the key text for Zion Baptist Church has been: 'My grace is sufficient for you, for my power is made perfect in weakness' (2 Corinthians 12.9).

A story from Wales

Coal was mined around Penrhys, Rhondda from the 1860s but in the late 1960s it became known mainly as a community suffering the worst excesses of planners. In the 1980s, 90% of its population was on housing benefit; many residents were third-generation unemployed people. In 1989 the church followed a traditional pattern of church life. Led by a United Reformed Church minister, its ten members asked if there were other patterns more suited to their circumstances. A new style has emerged. There are a café, a launderette, and a homework room for youngsters. Four flats house the minister, an education worker, a music student, and overseas students. Fifty people form discussion groups. Outside help, and the members' own growing confidence, created a church community within the Penrhys community. For example, when in 1997 residents heard their houses were to be destroyed, the church shared in an action group to stir an unresponsive local council.

Reflection

After sharing these stories continue the discussion begun in earlier weeks of this course on the needs of the local community(ies) represented in the group.

- How can the churches, being equipped for tomorrow, work together to respond to local community needs?

- In what ways are the local churches already becoming 'bridges of hope'?

- What is already happening locally? How can we support it? Are there unmet needs?

The group may wish to continue to meet and to commit themselves to turn their reflections into action.

Sharing the hope *(5 minutes)*

Get the group to suggest the content of a short letter to their churches, highlighting some of the problems the group has identified and the ways in which they might be tackled. There will not be time to complete the letter in the session so decide how the final copy of the letter can be produced and then communicated to the churches, e.g. to church officers, magazine editors, Churches Together, or by a request to visit each church to deliver the letter.

Closing worship *(10 minutes)*

Eternal God,
In deep gratitude, we gather together our prayers
for and to those with whom you have united us in our Lenten meetings,
not only in thought and action
but in your heavenly household.
Now, in this time and place,
faced with a world we sometimes delight in,
   sometimes wonder at,
   sometimes despair of,
may your guiding light illuminate our paths,
as you lit the paths of saints who lived before us.

Pull our eyes heavenward and root our feet firmly on the ground
that we may live in this world as your saints –
signposts of your love,
   your good news,
   your kingdom in the making.
And in all this, keep us attentive
to the will of the one who calls us,
who desires us,
who has a purpose for us. Amen.

© WGRG Iona Community (adapted)

Light the candle which is already on the table and slowly pass it from hand to hand around the group as a sign of commitment to each other in the calling to be saints together. This can be done in silence or by using the following affirmation:

When passing the candle: **Christ is in our midst!**

When receiving the candle: **He is and always will be!**

Closing prayer

Leader	From where we are to where you need us,
All	**Jesus, now lead on.**
Leader	From the security of what we know to the adventure of what you will reveal,
All	**Jesus, now lead on.**
Leader	To refashion the fabric of this world until it takes on the shape of your kingdom,
All	**Jesus, now lead on.**
Leader	Because good things have been prepared for those who love God,
All	**Jesus, now lead on.**

© WGRG Iona Community

Appendix 1

Building bridges of hope together

Some of the stories in this ecumenical Lent course come from a learning process called 'Building Bridges of Hope', which has brought together hundreds of Christians from a range of communities who have one thing in common: they are seeking, in different ways, to find fresh patterns of witness and service in a fast-changing world.

Over a period of three years 40 congregations across England, Scotland, Ireland and Wales have engaged in an in-depth process of companionship and review. They were chosen because they formed a cross-section from different Christian traditions and local settings. None claimed to be 'special' or 'extraordinary'. But all were (and are) committed to seeking personal and social transformation for themselves and for the communities in which they are placed.

'Building Bridges of Hope' (BBH) is an ecumenical event, not a new package or prescription. It is an invitation to churches at all levels (local, regional and national) to discover the key factors that assist health, engagement and effectiveness in Christian mission. This is currently being done through a network of 'pilot projects' that will show new ways forward for churches in a changing world.

One of the key BBH findings has been that Christians and church communities develop best when accompanied and supported. It is through 'journeying with the saints', both individually and corporately, that energy, wisdom and insight come. This requires long-term commitment, preparedness to see ourselves through fresh eyes, readiness to change, willingness to be looking outwards, and the ability to find appropriate resources as we concentrate on what is most important in our journey.

All this sounds daunting. But while the media talk of church decline, in many communities the sparks and structures of regeneration are emerging. For those who want to know more, and to work out what it means to be 'called to be saints' in a particular time and place, there are several resources available:

- A **video** called *Bridges to Build* puts BBH into story form. It lets you hear the authentic voices of Christians from a range of communities – inner city, suburban and rural, younger and older, white and black. This comes with a work booklet with study material and suggestions, and links to further help – not least the Association of Building-Bridges Churches (ABC). It can be purchased through http://www.chbookshop.co.uk. (Search: Bridges to Build)

- A new popular **book of stories** from Building Bridges congregations and communities is also being written. *Changing Churches*, by Jeanne Hinton (CTBI Publications), will be published in February 2002. If you want to be told when it is available, drop an email to bbh@ctbi.org.uk.

- For further information about Building Bridges of Hope, please visit our website at http://www.ctbi.org.uk/bbh.

Appendix 2

Saints in some of the different traditions

Introduction

In November 1999 CTBI organized a Consultation at Ushaw College, Durham with the title 'A Weekend with Abbess Hild and the Northern Saints'. On the first morning there was a conference discussion with speakers on the theme: 'What do we mean by a "saint", and how do our different denominations define and recognize this kind of person?' Four speakers spoke for their churches and a brief summary of what they said is given below. Their words should not be taken as official pronouncements of the churches they represented but simply as records from one specific conference.

Roman Catholic (Dr Sarah Boss)

In the New Testament the word 'saint' referred to all those who heard the gospel and were leading holy lives. From the time of the early Christian martyrs there was a growth in the honouring of saints beginning with those who had actually died for their faith. For some time saints were recognized by popular acclaim but then local churches began to exercise some control.

From the thirteenth century onwards, the approval of the Pope had to be given for a new saint to be declared and there is now a careful process of canonization. An extensive investigation has to be carried out to establish that s/he has performed an outstanding deed of holiness or lived a very holy life. Evidence of miracles is investigated. The Church first declares the person 'Blessed'. Later they can be declared 'Saint' if there is continuing support and further evidence of miracles. People become attached to special saints and ask their prayers for particular forms of help, both spiritual and practical.

Orthodox (Mrs Gillian Crow)

We are all as Christians called to be saints. Orthodoxy understands this to be the aim of the Christian life. We are all part of the Communion of Saints.

51

In the early church, the martyrs came to be especially honoured and their tombs and relics regarded as particularly sacred. After them came the Confessors and the Desert Fathers and Mothers.

The process by which people come to be declared officially as saints begins with popular acclaim. This springs from their holiness and good deeds. It may involve miracles but miracles are not necessary for a person to become a saint. This popular recognition will be investigated and verified by the local bishop. If the memory and the veneration spread, it will be investigated and verified by the local Church, e.g. the Russian Church, the Church of Greece, etc. If a saint is accepted by a local Church, s/he is then accepted by all Orthodox Churches even if they are not included in all the local calendars.

The Orthodox, conscious of being one big family of believers, living and departed, also ask the saints for prayers. All Orthodox Christians have patron saints, whose name they are given at baptism and for whom they will have a special devotion.

Anglican (Rt Revd Alan Smithson – Bishop of Jarrow)

Bishop Alan stressed that for Anglicans the biblical basis that we are all called to be saints is vitally important. There is no biblical evidence that certain people are special saints in a particular way and are in a special position in the afterlife. Yet at the Reformation, Cranmer had retained the names of biblical people such as St John or St Nathaniel etc. for commemoration as 'red letter' saints within the Christian calendar. They were each given their own collect and readings at Holy Communion. In the 1920s when there was a call in the Anglican Communion for the commemoration of more saints, it was made clear by the Lambeth Conference of Bishops that saints were not to be invoked but were to be regarded as 'ensamples of godly life'. In other words they were to be honoured as good examples to be followed in living the Christian life, and God is to be petitioned that we may be helped to follow their good example. (Bishop Alan recognized that some Anglicans do invoke saints but suggested that this is done as members of one fellowship. Veneration belongs to God alone.)

New saints are added to the calendar from local situations, dioceses and national churches where they have come to be honoured and respected. Within the Anglican Communion saints are added to the calendar and liturgical provision is made for them by the decision of the General Synods of the various Provinces. There is a common core of generally recognized saints.

The Quaker tradition (Anne Smith)

The word 'saint' is a translation of the Greek word *hagios* meaning 'a holy person' and this was something which all members of the early church were called to be. Quakers traditionally rejected all titles, were against hierarchical structures and therefore opposed any idea of saints, which suggested a hierarchical heaven.

There is no corporate Quaker body which canonizes saints. There is, however, a mechanism that highlights people who have demonstrated exceptionally that God is within themselves.

> Our custom of writing testimonies to the grace of God as shown in the lives of Friends provides us with a wealth of material showing ordinary Friends living out their faith from day to day. The testimonies show us that, whatever our circumstances, God can be present with us, and they encourage us each to be faithful to our calling ... If the testimony is likely to be of benefit to the society as a whole, it may be forwarded to Yearly Meeting. This should not, however, be an automatic decision. Its value as an inspiration to other Friends is not dependent only on its relevance in a wider rather than a local context.
>
> *Quaker Faith and Practice* (1995), chapter 18

Each year testimonies are written and a number of these are forwarded to Yearly Meeting to be included in the text that informs that Meeting. A testimony is pieced together through memoirs and minutes of Quaker meetings, but it is important to remember that the purpose of the testimony is not to honour the person but to give thanks for the grace of God as demonstrated in the life of that person.

The Reformed Churches and Free Churches

As these four comments were discussed in the CTBI group planning this 2002 Lent Course, the Revd Donald Hilton (Moderator of the group and a United Reformed Church minister) and the Revd Martin Johnstone (a Church of Scotland minister) affirmed that the background of the Friends' statement – though not the formalized Quaker process – was comparable to that of the other Free Churches in stressing that 'saint' is a biblical description of all believers both individually and as the body of the Church, both in its universal and local expression.

In the New Testament 'saint' is hardly ever used in the singular. It knows nothing of *Saint* Paul or *Saint* Mark, except as part of the living 'communion of saints' which transcends earthly distinctions of race, gender, hierarchy, wealth or poverty, or social distinction. For example, in the nineteenth and early twentieth century, Nonconformity in Wales frequently used *sant* (plural, *saint*) to refer to the faithful people of God, especially the elderly. It implied 'steadfastness in the Faith', e.g. *yr hen sant, John Jones* – the old saint, John Jones.

Most Free Church people would approach the traditional 'sacred sites', 'relics', and processes of canonization with a degree of scepticism and, whilst honouring those believers who in present and previous times have been outstanding in their Christian example, would not pray to or through them, believing that each person has direct access to God, without priest or saint, through Jesus Christ.

Conclusion

These summaries show that in spite of our differences over canonization and invocation the various churches do hold some things in common about saints. We all agree that all Christians are 'called to be saints', that we can be inspired by the stories of people's lives and witness, and that 'community' is an essential element in any response to the question, 'What do we mean by "saint"?'

These views, which we hold in common, form part of the basis and the inspiration for this Lent course.

Appendix 3

The concept of pilgrimage

The third strand which underlies this Lent course is the theme of pilgrimage. This theme runs throughout the Scriptures. Abraham was called to leave his home in Ur and travel as a pilgrim into the unknown in search of a new land and a new knowledge of God. He set out to go to the land of Canaan and when he came to that land he still journeyed on.

The first five books of the Bible, the Pentateuch, are books of reflection on the journey of the Hebrews from slavery in Egypt to the Promised Land. The reflection led the writers to see that the Hebrew/Jewish people were called to a continuing journey to get to know God and grow to be his people. For Christians those ancient longings are fulfilled in Jesus, but he also travelled light and called his followers to journey with him. The early Christians were known as the people of 'the Way'.

In the Middle Ages, when the Christian Church began to weigh itself down with buildings, the longing to join in pilgrimages also grew and the cathedrals, with their shrines of the saints, became centres of pilgrimage. The pilgrimages were fun as well as holy and we see something of this in Chaucer's *Canterbury Tales*. For the pilgrims, the journey and the companionship were as important as to arrive at the goal.

At the Reformation the good baby of pilgrimages was often thrown out with the bathwater of superstition. A free thinker like Bunyan, however, could still write in prison a book like *Pilgrim's Progress*, with the theme of the journey to heaven and the overcoming of temptation.

Today ecumenical pilgrimages are increasingly seen as a way of helping us to travel together both on the actual journey and in our life as churches together. In 1999 the European Co-ordinating Group for Mission and Renewal reminded us that we are all called to be pilgrims as Christian life is a journey with Christ, from death to life, from separation to reconciliation, from despair to hope. They organized pilgrimages across Europe in 2000 and 2001. In these pilgrimages people learned to travel light, to share the journey with one another and to give a common witness to a living faith in our time. As Christians we also need to learn to do this in our Christian life from birth to death, from time to eternity. On our pilgrim way we can be encouraged by the example of other Christians past and present. We hope that this Lent course *Called to be saints* will provide some of that encouragement.

Evaluation form

At the end of this course we would be grateful if each group would fill in the following evaluation form and return it to Lent 2002 Evaluation, CTBI, Inter-Church House, 35-41 Lower Marsh, London SE1 7SA.

Your group

Our group met in...(*house, town, village*)

How many members were there in your group? ....

Which Churches (denominations) did they come from?..

....

In the sections below you are provided with some statements followed by 1, 2, 3, 4. Please circle:
- 1   if you **strongly agree** with the statement
- 2   if you **agree** with the statement
- 3   if you **disagree** with the statement
- 4   if you **strongly disagree** with the statement.

Session 1

This was an interesting and helpful session	1	2	3	4
It was valuable to re-think what we mean by 'saint'	1	2	3	4
The use of various maps was interesting	1	2	3	4
The Bible reading and discussion was helpful	1	2	3	4
The prayers were meaningful	1	2	3	4

Session 2

This was an interesting and helpful session	1	2	3	4
The prayers at the beginning and end were an inspiration	1	2	3	4
The stories showed how where we live affects discipleship	1	2	3	4
The Bible reflection was interesting	1	2	3	4
The session helped us to recognize our call to be saints	1	2	3	4

Session 3

This was an interesting and helpful session	1	2	3	4
We enjoyed the time-line activity and found it helpful	1	2	3	4
We learnt a lot from the Syrophoenician woman	1	2	3	4
We valued the discussion about Diana and Mother Teresa	1	2	3	4
We valued time to reflect on being saints ourselves	1	2	3	4

Session 4

This was an interesting and helpful session	1	2	3	4
We found it novel to reflect on the 'saint' behind Paul	1	2	3	4
We enjoyed this way of using stories	1	2	3	4
It was good to have a varied choice of stories	1	2	3	4
We welcomed the chance to speak of inspiring people	1	2	3	4

Session 5

This was an interesting and helpful session	1	2	3	4
The amount of material was right for the time available	1	2	3	4
The Bible study was exciting and worthwhile	1	2	3	4
It was encouraging to hear about communities of hope	1	2	3	4
The closing worship was inspirational	1	2	3	4

General

On the whole the Lent course was of the right depth	1	2	3	4
The course nurtured our growth in holiness	1	2	3	4
The course helped us to understand our calling to be saints	1	2	3	4
We would hope to use a CTBI course again	1	2	3	4

Please add any further comments you wish to make.

Acknowledgements

The publisher gratefully acknowledges permission to reproduce copyright material in this publication. Every effort has been made to trace and contact copyright holders. If there are any inadvertent omissions we apologize to those concerned and will ensure that a suitable acknowledgement is made at the next reprint.

The Scripture quotations contained herein are from The New Revised Standard Version of the Bible, Anglicized Edition, copyright © 1989, 1995 by the Division of Christian Education of the National Council of the Churches of Christ in the United States of America, and are used by permission. All rights reserved.

The Archbishops' Council: for the collect (adapted) for Pentecost 2 from *The Alternative Service Book 1980*.

The Catholic Institute for International Relations: for part of the story of Enoe from *Life out of Death: The Feminine Spirit in El Salvador*, by Marigold Best and Pamela Hussey, 1996.

CYTÛN: for the two verses in Welsh of the hymns of Ann Griffiths, as published in their book *Seasons of Glory*, 1997.

David Fox: for his translations of two of Ann Griffiths' hymns, as published in *Seasons of Glory*, CYTÛN, 1997.

HarperCollins Publishers: for the extract from *Marie: A Story from Enniskillen*, by Gordon Wilson and Alf McCreary, 1990.

Donald Hilton: for the prayers beginning 'Gracious God, present in every place' and 'Glory to you, O God'.

The Iona Community: for the following prayers from material prepared by the Wild Goose Resources Group: 'Gathered at God's table', 'Eternal God, in deep gratitude' and 'From where we are'.

Acknowledgements

Janet Morley: for the litany beginning 'For all the Saints' from *Bread of Tomorrow*, SPCK and Christian Aid, 1992.

Oxford University Press: for some verses of the hymn beginning 'Glory to thee, O Lord', by H. C. A. Gaunt.

Transworld Publications: for the extract from *Some Other Rainbow*, by John McCarthy and Jill Morrell, 1993.

Front cover photographs:

CAFOD: Oscar Romero, copyright © Joe Fish.

Church Missionary Society: Archbishop Janani Luwum.

E & E Picture Library/ D. Burrow: St David with harp, St Mungo's Museum, Glasgow.

Mary Evans Picture Library Ltd: St Andrew, unnamed artist in *Collection of Miniatures*; St Brigid, Cayley Robinson in *Saints and their Stories*.

Edith Reyntiens: St Hilda. Used by permission of the artist.

The Salvation Army International Heritage Centre: William and Catherine Booth.